Sports Massage for Horses

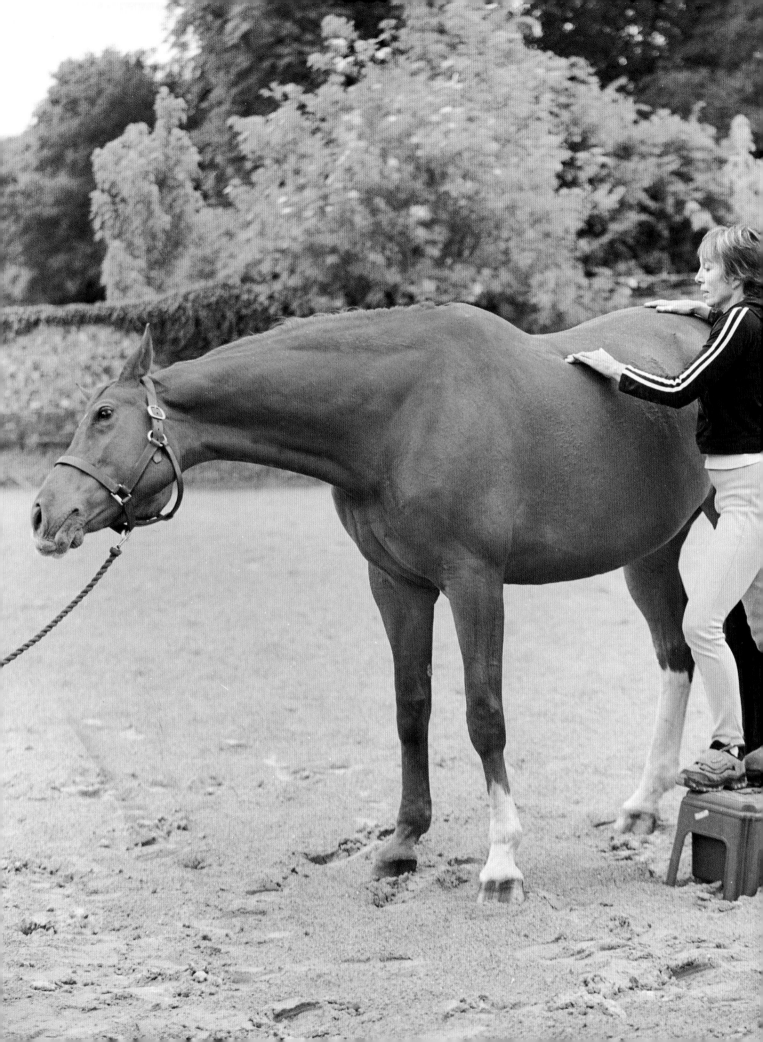

Sports Massage for Horses

PENNIE HOOPER JMI, SMT

TRAFALGAR SQUARE PUBLISHING

North Pomfret, Vermont

First published in the United States of America in 2005 by
Trafalgar Square Publishing, North Pomfret, Vermont 05053

Printed in Singapore by KHL Printing Co Pte Ltd

Published simultaneously in the UK by Kenilworth Press Ltd

ISBN-13: 978-1-57076-325-0
ISBN-10: 1-57076-325-9

Library of Congress Control Number: 2005905134

Design by Paul Saunders
Layout by Kenilworth Press

Author's Note
All the information contained in this book stems from the author's personal
experience of using sports massage on her own horses, and on those
belonging to other people, with the supervision or knowledge of the horse
owner's veterinarian.

Disclaimer
This book is not to be used in place of veterinary care and expertise.
No responsibility can be accepted by the author, publishers or distributors of
this book for the application of any of the enclosed information in practice.

10 9 8 7 6 5 4 3 2 1

Contents

ACKNOWLEDGEMENTS

My thanks to Mary Wanless for believing in me.

To Sorrel Warwick (and her horse Sport – the one with the big white blaze) for her unending support throughout my career.

To Mel Pollard at Sauce Design for being totally unflappable in the production of the muscle diagrams for this book.

To Bob Atkins, whose lovely photos adorn this book.

To my illustrator Kristine Nason for turning my scribbles into informative and/or humorous art, and Dianne Breeze for her expert transformation of photographs into line drawings for the comparative exercises.

To Roger Meacock, BVSc, MRCVS, whose pioneering veterinary treatments have helped where conventional methods have failed.

To Lesley Gowers and all at Kenilworth Press.

To Melanie Brown and her lovely horse Fifi, who is featured in this book.

To Line Hansen, Darryl Harper, Jo Stevens and Diane Rickard, whose help has been invaluable in getting this book written.

And lastly, to my children, Toby and Bea, for understanding when I have said, 'Just got to go and write this down . . .'

Thank you all.

PENNIE HOOPER

Foreword

by Mary Wanless

I first met Pennie Hooper in the early 1990s when she came as a participant on one of my 'Ride with your Mind' riding courses. After attending a couple of these, she also completed a teacher training course, after which she quietly admitted to me that she didn't actually want to teach riding; what she really wanted to do was to massage horses. This was said rather sheepishly (quite out of character for Pennie) because she had, apparently, been met with hysterical laughter whenever she had voiced her dream.

It seems that I was the first person to take her seriously, and also to point her in the right direction. Pennie was already qualified as a human sports massage therapist, and she had come into a little money, which she wanted to spend on training to work with horses – but where? The UK, at that time, did not offer much in the way of training opportunities, so it was to America that she went. It took three attempts for her to find the approach that worked with her sharp intellect, and her need to know both how and why. (Interestingly, most of the body workers I know do not now practise the first modality they trained in. It seems to take a bit of hands-on experience and some getting to know the field before they find an approach they truly believe in.)

The Jack Meagher Institute offered Pennie a rigorous training and the chance to be apprenticed to the best in the USA. With some experience under her belt, she came back to the UK and opened her practice. Every month she came for one day on my courses, massaging the participants' horses and offering them her diagnostic insights, as well as some stretches and simple massage movements that they could continue doing at home. Her analogies with the human body have helped people to understand just what their horses go through as they carry saddle and rider and respond to the demands of dressage and jumping. Unfortunately, this includes both the true demands of athletic endeavour and the false demands of the impossible contortions that we (unknowingly) force them into.

Ten years later, Pennie still comes to all of my courses and she also massages horses for some very well-known riders and trainers. She is now one of those people who genuinely has ten years' worth of experience, rather than one year of experience repeated ten times! She is the first to admit that the horses themselves have taught her more about how and where they need to be massaged than any human could ever teach her. I have watched many horses (my own included) tell her 'left a bit Pennie, that's it, just there ... now down a bit'. I have watched them push back against her, saying 'more pressure, Pennie!' as they all but flatten her tiny body against the wall! This can be both comical and endearing. Because she listens and follows their lead, Pennie is one of the most popular people in town. From a human as well as an equine viewpoint, her perception and application have made her an exceptionally good therapist, as well as an excellent diagnostician.

Ten years on, the UK is a very different place. No one, I think, would now be laughed out of court for saying that they wanted to massage horses. Even old school vets and horsemasters are appreciating the grey area between sound and lame, where the many 'walking wounded' horses keep soldiering on. Often, this is without complaint – and those who do complain are too often dismissed as 'difficult' or 'nappy'. But our options for the twenty-first century have moved far beyond 'bute it or shoot it'; to those who see and feel more than the average punter, the body speaks of its history, its limitations and its longing to be whole and pain-free.

Like every bodyworker I know whose practice includes work on humans and horses, Pennie would rather massage horses any day of the week – even, and perhaps particularly, the 'difficult' ones. This says something about what horses, as opposed to people, give back to their therapists, and how thankful they are for some help. Whether our horses are competitive athletes, or 'happy hackers', we as riders have a responsibility to keep them in the best shape we can. No one performs well when limited by pain, or even by restrictions so familiar that they are no longer noticed. While the mind remains in blissful ignorance, the body must find ways to compensate – adding yet more contortions to its repertoire until the final result is an injury it really will notice.

Each in our own small way, Pennie and I aim to make the world a better place for horses. More than anything else, this means educating people so that they too appreciate the inherent flaws in the equine as well as the human body, and the price our horses can pay for the enormous gifts that they give us.

Introduction

By nature, horses are flight animals, designed to evade predators and move swiftly at speeds of up to 40 miles per hour; their eyes are set at the sides of their head, facilitating almost 360-degree vision; they can sleep standing up; and by grazing and moving in herds they benefit from sharing many eyes and ears, constantly alert to danger.

Domestication of the horse has had a fundamental effect upon the history and development of mankind. We have harnessed the horse's qualities of strength, stamina and compliance, to use him as a beast of burden and for transport. He has had his place in revolutionising methods of farming, warfare and travel. On the timeline of our association with this amazing animal, it is only recently (and as his usefulness in traditional areas declined) that we have begun to appreciate and exploit the horse's potential as an athlete and partner in our recreational pursuits.

We can train horses to run faster, jump higher and perform the balletic movements of dressage for our entertainment and pleasure – a rider in control, testing and perfecting our skills. But as we sit comfortably on our horse's back, how often do we stop to consider how comfortable our horse is? It should be obvious that when we ask a horse to perform a task, communication will be made easier through having some understanding of the horse's mind and his physical needs.

By using human comparisons (in my 'comparative exercises'), I hope to help you to empathise with your horse, to get a sense of what he feels. As you can see from the illustration overleaf, horses and humans are quite similar structurally, and both commonly suffer from low back pain and problems involving the shoulder and neck areas.

This understanding should enable you to work in synergy with your horse and promote better performance for both you and him.

Physical distress leads to mental distress. Often horses presenting with mental stress will be those who have, and may have had for some time, a great deal of physical pain due to muscular dysfunction. These horses are often misunderstood and deemed to be 'naughty' by their owners.

As we become more aware that horses do indeed possess and exhibit

Comparison between human
and equine skeletal structure.
Red shading depicts common
areas of pain.

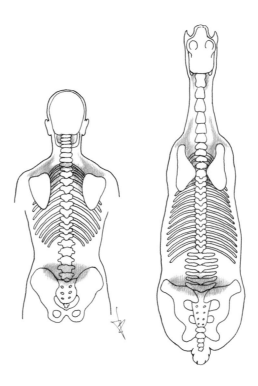

some human characteristics, our attitudes are changing, encouraging us to look behind the behavioural problems for a cure.

In my own experience I have seen countless horses change from being shut down, non-responsive and non co-operative to becoming user-friendly, confident and eventually happy once the physical side of the problem has been dealt with.

Sports massage is not necessarily a cure in itself, however, and it usually takes a team of therapists to get the best results out of any equine athlete, including osteopaths, remedial farriers, saddlers, equine dentists and animal behaviourists, to help the animal attain maximum performance. Sports massage can identify a potential or developing problem before it becomes chronic.

Equine Sports Massage Explained

CORRECT MUSCLE USAGE

A horse's natural centre of gravity is slightly behind the shoulder and approximately one third of the way down his body. In order to accommodate the weight of a rider, we need to ask the horse to adjust his centre of gravity and balance. If, however, we fail to do this, the horse's weight and power will come mainly from the front – in riding terms this is known as working on the forehand – and your horse will develop large muscular shoulders, rather like those of a weight-lifter. At the same time his back muscles will tend to be under-developed or weak – which we refer to as having no 'top-line'– and the gluteal muscles of the hindquarters will also remain weak, as the horse is pulling himself along from the front end, rather than pushing himself forwards from behind. Lightness at the front of the horse will be lost and he will no longer be able to turn quickly on his hindquarters. The unfortunate horse is using only about one third of his power, as he is employing the shoulders for both impulsion and steering.

To illustrate the point, look at the photos of the two cars. See how their shapes are quite different. Can you tell at a glance which is the more

Which car would **you** prefer to drive?

powerful? Yes! But how do you know that? Most cars with big engines have rear-wheel drive; as you accelerate, the weight of the car moves backwards, putting more weight on the rear tyres and making it lighter to steer at the front. With rear-wheel drive you are pushing rather than pulling. You have more control through corners as the wide tyres at the heavy rear end grip the road. Horses, just like cars, function much better when pushing from behind, i.e. when being ridden from the back to the front!

The aim of training is to modify the horse's physical development and to produce an animal fit to carry a rider, without hindrance to his natural athletic capabilities – that is, where the front is light and used for steering, and the hindquarters produce the power. Look at the examples (opposite). Can you work out which horse is powered from behind? The horse in the top photo has more muscle covering the shoulders, because he pulls himself along. The horse in the lower photo has a much more even muscle tone throughout his body; the front and the back look similar in terms of muscular development. Which horse do you think is more comfortable both to ride and in himself?

Using the following comparative exercise we can explore what it feels like for a horse that is working on the forehand.

Comparative Exercise 1

● Stand up straight, lock your knees and stick out your bottom and your chest. Now bend over, letting your arms hang as low as possible. Next (and here's the best bit), try taking a few steps. Not easy, eh?

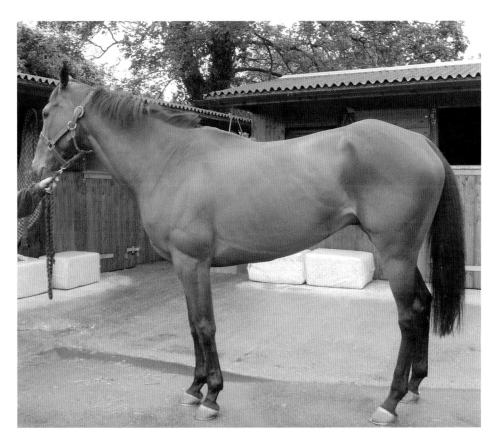

Which horse would **you** prefer to ride? Look at the over-development of the shoulders and how much more defined they are on the bay horse compared to those of the chestnut. This is because the bay horse is pulling rather than pushing.

● Now we will start all over again. This time, your back is not hollow; don't lock your knees; don't stick your bottom and chest out; bend over again and take a few steps. Now you are using more back more efficiently, I think you will notice how much easier it is! So now you can understand how inefficient and uncomfortable it is for your horse when he is working on the forehand.

Another problem caused by moving around incorrectly is wear and tear on the horse's joints. When more weight bears down (is applied) on the front end, the forelegs are forced to take too much strain and the horse may begin to experience a higher incidence of tendon problems and sore shins, and he may go lame in front more often. Moreover, because he is unable to use his back muscles effectively, he will not develop a 'top-line'. The horse needs to be relaxed and able to flex through his back properly, otherwise the top-line will effectively be locked and rigid and muscular dysfunction will occur and re-occur – his back will be weak. The horse won't really be using his back end to power himself forwards, therefore the angle of the pelvis will tend to be shallow and the hindquarters will look underdeveloped. This is just plain crazy, as this is where the horse's real power – the engine – lies! You now have a situation similar to driving along in a car in slow traffic with the clutch pedal half way down.

The back muscles should work in unison with the belly muscles, assisting the development of the top-line, which is fundamental to the term we call 'engagement'. Translated roughly, this means the horse is using its belly muscles in unison with his back musculature to produce more effective and powerful forward motion. Do you ever see a human athlete with a saggy belly? A horse with slack belly muscles will encounter the same problems as

a human. Can you recognise him? Yes! We've all seen him down our local! Hello, 'Beer-Belly Horse'! Or how about 'Gym Horse'? He is the one that goes to the gym three or four times a week, and is generally fit and athletic.

Both horses will encounter muscular strain through training, but the 'beer-belly' horse will suffer more problems, as his muscles are not working in unison, causing the over-use of some muscle groups.

Sports massage is possibly the most effective way to identify muscular strain, and combined with correct training it also assists the remedy. The techniques used enable the musculature to relax, therefore stopping the cycle of stiff muscles changing to damaged muscles, and help to correct the original problem.

REPETITIVE STRAIN INJURY (RSI) EXPLAINED

Most people at some time will have experienced an RSI as writer's cramp. This may have happened during the writing of a long letter or an essay, when the very specialised muscles used for writing became fatigued. If this were to continue on a daily basis eventually the tendons of the hand would become contracted, affecting the joint mobility and producing pain and stiffness.

At no time would you think of changing your pen into the other hand to provide relief – writing is such a specialised task that the other hand could not take over, and this lack of an alternative method of working aggravates the RSI problem. It is the same for horses, except that their tasks are chosen by you, the rider, even if your horse's own RSI makes the task difficult. If your horse, for example, starts to refuse at a fence that he managed perfectly well last season, or resists switching leads, he may be trying to tell you something. In my experience, horses are compliant, docile creatures, and learning to recognise these hints may help you to detect an RSI.

Any horse that is involved in sport or training at any level, will be asked to perform certain movements repetitively, and it is this repetition that causes a chain of events that will ultimately produce an RSI.

To function smoothly, a muscle must be able to contract and relax, with its fibres gliding and folding over each other. It is when the muscle becomes stressed that this process begins to dysfunction.

The normal response for any muscle under stress is to tighten, or to become contracted. Anyone who has ever had backache will recognise this response as a general stiffness, usually in the lower back. Once the muscle becomes stiff, it becomes inefficient at eliminating waste products, creating a build-up of toxins in the muscle tissue. This in turn makes the muscle less able to collect oxygen. Once the contraction and relaxation of the muscle is impaired, a never-ending loop is created – no oxygen equals no elimination of waste products, and the oxygen depletion then leads to pathological changes deep within the muscle tissue. And so 'overuse syndrome' begins. The muscle will begin to change its pathology at a microscopic level, leading to the formation of muscular spasms (leading to pain), which can be felt as tightening, or, as it gets worse, as hard, nodular, localised, contracted muscular bundles. (You will often be able to feel these in your own shoulders, above the shoulder blade.)

Often no discomfort is felt until the problem reaches a critical level. Therefore the rider is unaware of the problem and exercise continues, placing greater strain on the damaged muscle fibres. However, because the contraction and relaxation process of the muscle has diminished, this will have an effect on the horse's range of movement. Shortened muscles equate to shortened strides and mis-timed fences.

The tendon is the last link in the chain to be affected as it gains its protection from the adjacent muscle tissues, which have ninety per cent more elasticity than the tendon. Thus, for example, if the shoulder muscles are tight, the tightening will pass down into the muscles of the foreleg and eventually into the tendon.

Another way a horse can receive a muscular injury will be from a sudden impact injury, which may happen if, for instance, your horse takes a tumble at a fence. The rider may not pick up on the problem but there may well be muscular damage which, if left untreated, could lead to the same symptoms as described above.

Horses are very clever at throwing us off the scent, too! As they have four legs, rather than two, it is not always easy for the rider to gauge where or how the horse has been affected by muscular damage, as most muscle damage is so insidious to begin with that it is hard to detect. It is also quite common for the problem to arise as a secondary issue on the diagonally opposite leg. For example, a horse that has a stiff near-fore will often load the off-hind to compensate. Most horses have one rein that they are stiffer on and it is often a useful place to start to look for spasm and muscle contraction. Tightened muscle tissue spotted early enough, can prevent the development of many chronic joint conditions if the stress patterns are identified and treated.

GETTING STARTED

When massaging a horse for the first time I usually find that a good place to start is on the shoulders, as most horses are used to being patted there. If, though, you find a better place to start, that's fine – there are no fixed rules.

It's a good idea to give your horse a complete sports massage about once a month. This way, after time, you will begin to recognise the difference between smooth, correctly functioning muscle tissue and contracted, hard, malfunctioning muscle tissue. An all-over massage should take roughly 45 minutes, but if you want to concentrate on specific areas this is fine, just remember not to stay too long on one spot or you could risk bruising the muscle.

Choose an environment that the horse is familiar with, and have him on a loose contact with a handler present. (The photos used in this book were all taken outdoors because most stables are fairly gloomy.)

CAUTION

It is essential to have a handler during your first massage session, as they can keep an eye on your horse's reactions. Have your horse on a loose lead line, as this is safer for both you, and the handler. This way, if he doesn't like what you are doing, he has the option of moving. If you hold him too tightly, he may panic if the pressure you are using doesn't feel good to him and he cannot escape it.

I use a rubber groomer on some muscles. The best ones I have found are dog groomers, as rubber horse groomers tend to be too stiff. Do be careful,

Above: This is the softer type of groomer that I prefer.
Left: Micropore™ tape helps to protect your hands.

though, as some horses have very fine coats and over-using a groomer in any area can cause the coat to thin out.

Bear in mind that the groomer is a tool and does not have the sensitivity of your fingers. Make the strokes slow, rhythmical and circular. Most horses tolerate this well, but some do dislike it. Over time, your horse will begin to give you clues as to what he likes most, and how much pressure you can use on him. Throughout this book, you will find tips on where and when to use the groomer.

The way this grooming box is designed makes it less liable to tip over.

Having a box to stand on can be very useful, even if you have a small horse. The extra height allows you to use more downward pressure when applying massage techniques to the horse's back.

Choose something sturdy. Milk-crates, being rather light, are prone to flip over if your horse makes a sudden movement. I use a grooming box, inside which I put bits, groomers, books, Micropore™ tape and an invoice book – all of which makes it rather heavy, but it has never flipped over!

TIP

I always use Micropore™ tape on my fingers, as firstly it helps to keep your nails cleaner, and secondly it protects the ends of your fingers, which can become sore, especially in the winter when the horse's coat is clipped.

CONTRA-INDICATIONS TO SPORTS MASSAGE

- Sports massage should be applied only to horses that are not under veterinary treatment.

- If your horse is lame, call your vet.

- If you feel any areas of heat and/or swelling, call your vet.

- If your horse has a skin condition, wait until it clears up as you could spread it.

- If your horse has lymphangitis, or is prone to it, do not use sports massage EVER!

- If your horse is in foal, ask your vet's advice.

- If you suspect your horse has a temperature, do not massage him.

- Do not use sports massage on your horse directly after exercise. It should be done pre-exercise to prepare the muscles for working.

INTRODUCTION TO MASSAGE TECHNIQUES

Here is a game to play with some friends. Get an A4 pad of paper and a small piece of someone's hair (a single strand). One person places the hair under a sheet of paper, while the others must look away. The aim of the game is to find the hair using your fingers, rather than your eyes. You must try to find where it is and which way across the page it is lying. Then do this again, but using two sheets of paper, and so on. The person who is able to find the hair under the most sheets of paper is the winner, and also the most likely to be the best at massage!

In massage, the fingers become the eyes, feeling for the difference between a smooth, healthy muscle and a hardened, knotted one. Imagine running your fingers over a steak. Even with your eyes shut, you would know when your fingers came to a gristly bit! So, roughly, this is what we are looking for – something that interrupts the smooth flow of the muscle tissue.

If you have ever held a baby, you will know how soft and smooth they feel. This is the musculature body in a near perfect state, which, over time becomes less and less perfect. We all get sore shoulders from time to time, so start by feeling a friend's shoulders to try out the techniques, looking for hardness and 'knots'. This may not be easy to begin with, so guide and prompt one another, taking turns over who gets the massage. Your 'feel' will improve the more you practice.

In equine sports massage I use two techniques. The first one, compression, is a deep twisting movement done with the heel of the hand. If you are using your right hand, start by using pressure from the thumb side, working your hand in a clockwise direction using the same firm pressure throughout the movement. Each compression should take a couple of seconds. Work along the muscle and back again, moving 2–3 centimetres (about an inch) at a time. This will help relax the muscle tissue before applying the second technique.

The second, and most penetrating movement, is cross-fibre friction. This can be done using your thumb, or first and second fingers, the second resting over the first, which gives more leverage. It is called cross-fibre

Compression, using heel of hand.

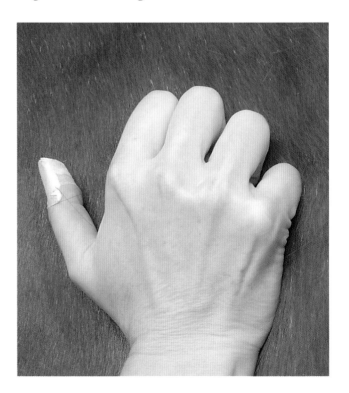

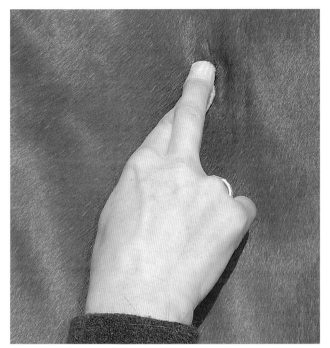
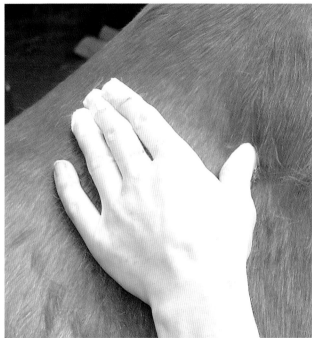

Cross-fibre friction, using forefinger and second finger (above left) and/or thumb (above right).

friction, as here you apply the technique across the grain of the muscle tissue where possible. The fingers move approximately 5 centimetres (2 inches) at a time, up and back repeatedly. The whole movement takes about two seconds, spending more time where you feel any hardening or knots. Done regularly this will begin to break down adhesions within the muscle tissue, thus allowing greater range of movement.

I have often been asked why I work at such speed. The answer is simple – this is the speed that horses themselves work at. If you have ever watched two horses grooming each other, you will know what I mean.

However, a point worth noting is that if you encounter any shivering or juddering it denotes areas of deep muscle spasm, and you will need to slow down here and not use a groomer. Any shivering area indicates extreme muscular contraction, which can be highly sensitised to pain, therefore slower movements are needed in order for the horse to relax and to let you work at a deeper level.

When you begin to perfect these techniques, your horse will want to groom you too. I cannot emphasise enough that practice is the key and perseverance is a virtue!

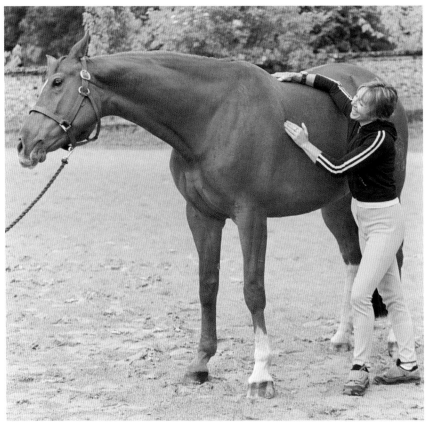

> **CAUTION**
>
> Never stand with
> your back towards
> your horse's head
> while applying
> massage
> techniques. You
> need to gauge the
> horse's reaction to
> the amount of
> pressure you are
> using and adjust
> the pressure
> accordingly.

ASSESSING HORSES

OBSERVING A MOVING HORSE

While most horse owners are used to feeling a horse move when riding, watching a horse move without a rider is not something most of us do regularly. It is worth making this a part of your stable routine, at least once a week.

> **TIP**
>
> Find a flat, even ground surface and ask a friend to lead your horse away from you at walk – ten to fifteen strides should be sufficient. I am often asked why this is done at walk. The answer is simple – it is when the muscles are at their most relaxed. At trot the muscles are more braced and it is harder to observe muscular tension.

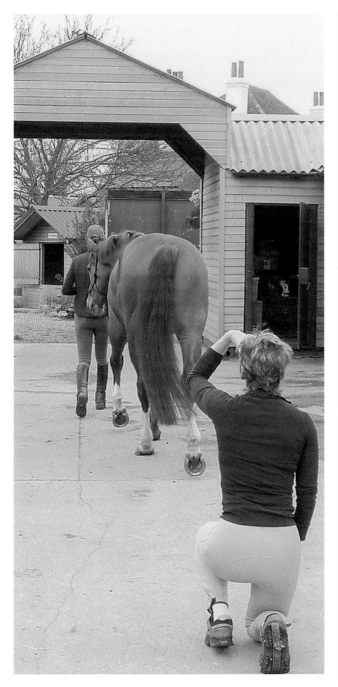
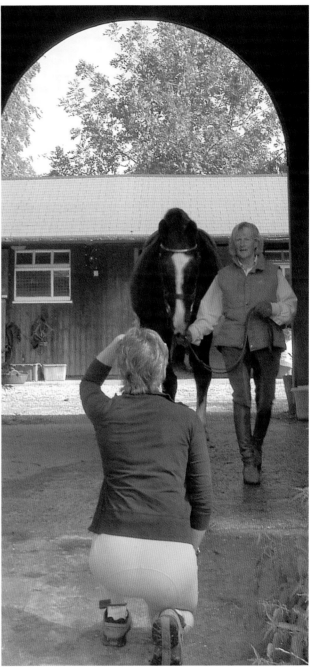

Observation is **so** important.

WHAT TO LOOK FOR WHEN THE HORSE IS WALKING AWAY FROM YOU

- Is the pelvis level? The hindquarters should look even, and the footfall of the hind legs should be in line with the front legs – i.e. moving in a straight line.

- Do the horse's hindquarters appear to be curled around to one side?

- Are the hocks moving evenly or does one look more restricted?

- Does the musculature of the hindquarters look even on both sides or does one side look more/less muscled up?

- Is the horse dragging one of his hind feet?

- Is he tracking up evenly?

WHAT TO LOOK FOR WHEN THE HORSE IS WALKING TOWARDS YOU

- Is his head over to one side?

- Is his neck over to one side?

- Do the shoulder muscles appear even?

- Are both forelegs moving evenly or does one leg appear to be more constricted?

To the untrained eye, some of these things may not be easy to spot to start with, but the more you watch your horse move from the ground, the easier it will become. Practice, practice, practice!

TIP

Make time to watch your horse being led. Do this before a competition and then again after it. This way, you will pick up on any muscle tightening as soon as it happens.

CHECKING FOR HEAT

Checking for heat is an important part of your massage routine, as it can indicate deeper problems. If you find any heated areas that last for more than a day or two, say after a competition, call in your vet and do not attempt to treat the area yourself, as you could worsen the problem.

If you suspect that you have a heated muscle, recheck it using the back of your hand rather than your palm. This is because the palm of your hand has more nerve endings and is therefore warmer. Hold your hand roughly 3 centimetres (just over an inch) from the suspect area. Any heat coming from the affected muscle should be more obvious, as this side of your hand is cooler.

Cold-water hosing, or ice, can treat minor problems. I use paper cups in which I have frozen water, so that as the ice melts you can roll down the paper cup and keep the iced surface in contact with the horse. One area, however, that I would not recommend treating with ice is the lower back – the area just behind the saddle. Ice causes the muscle tissue to contract, and any heat in this area will mean that your horse's back is already constricted, therefore you will only be adding to the problem by applying ice, thus making his sore back even tighter. Heat here needs to be checked by a vet and/or physiotherapist.

If you check your horse weekly, over time you will become more aware of his muscular condition. Consequently this will benefit your horse's performance because you will learn to recognise any muscular stress from the outset.

IMPORTANT

Please read the contra-indications (page 19) before you start to massage.

The Shoulder

Just as with humans, the horse's shoulders function much more efficiently the less restricted they are.

Comparative Exercise 2

- Stand up and walk across the room without moving your shoulders. How does this feel in your lower back? If your shoulders are not moving, you subconsciously stiffen the area around your waist, and you won't have given it a single thought. This is just one small example of how our muscles work in synergy – no one group can work without affecting another group, and so on through the whole body.

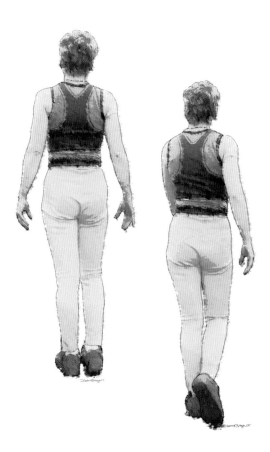

- Try the exercise again but let your shoulders swing. You should now feel much looser movement through your waist. If you look at the illustration on page 33 you will see that a saddle sits over the shoulders and major back muscles of the horse and, as we have seen in the above exercise, once the shoulder movement is compromised it will affect movement throughout the body.

Now let's look at the muscles of the shoulder one by one. By referring to the diagrams on pages 10 and 33 you will be able to see the similarities between where the muscles lie on a human and on a horse.

The black hatching indicates the thoracic trapezius muscle, the grey hatching is the cervical portion, and the white hatching indicates the rhomboid muscle.

TRAPEZIUS (Thoracic Part) AND RHOMBOIDS

Muscle action: To draw the shoulder forwards and backwards.

Problem: Losing ability over fences; loss of elasticity in all paces; shortened range of movement of forelegs.

Solution: Applying quite a firm pressure, using either compressions or cross-fibre friction, massage in a circular movement. If you go in firmly enough you may find tight lines of tissue running from the spinous processes to the top of the scapular bone. Massage for a total of 3–5 minutes each side. You will need to do this daily until you feel an improvement in your horse's performance.

TIP

It is a good idea to check these muscles after jumping, particularly if the ground is hard.

TRICEPS

Muscle action: To extend the elbow joint and flex the shoulder.

Problem: Dishing; shortened range of movement through forelegs; finding extended trot difficult.

Solution: You will need to work with a good firm pressure on this area for 5–10 minutes using compressions up and down the entire length of the muscle – until you feel tired is usually a good gauge! Follow this with some cross-fibre friction along the lower border of the scapular bone. Continue to do this daily until you notice an improvement in your horse's performance.

DELTOIDS

Muscle action: To flex the shoulder.

Problem: Shortened range of movement in forelegs; finding extended trot difficult; loss of ability over fences. Just as in humans, the upper end of the shoulder will feel hard if over-use is present.

Solution: This muscle lies behind the spine or the bony protuberance of the scapular bone. If, when you apply quite firm pressure, the muscle begins to tremor or the horse flinches or moves away, RSI is present.

Start by using cross-fibre friction, working in toward the spine of the scapular, followed by compressions. This should be done daily until you see an increase in the range of the horse's movement.

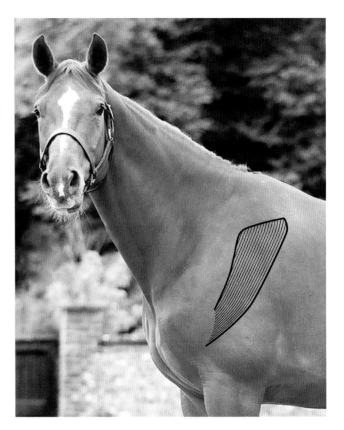

TIP

If this muscle is in spasm it is likely that the serratus ventralis and posterior pectorals will also be affected. Refer to the section on the ribcage and back for applied techniques.

SUPRASPINATUS AND INFRASPINATUS

Muscle action: To extend the shoulder and to bring the shoulder inwards towards the body. These are the deeper muscles of the shoulder, and they play an important part, particularly if you are working at advanced level dressage.

Problem: Lateral work lacks range of movement.

Solution: In the middle of the scapular bone you will find the 'spine' or 'dividing protuberance' – just like on a human. Using the heel of your hand, press firmly up and down the bone using compressions. If you come across any particularly hard knots of muscle tissue, work these areas using cross-fibre friction until you feel the muscular mass begin to soften. This should take about 5 minutes. Work on this daily until you notice an improvement in your horse's performance.

The Ribcage and Mid-Back

If you have ever experienced lower backache you will know how debilitating it is and how stiff you become – and grumpy too! It is the same for horses, and one of the main reasons I get called out.

Comparative Exercise 3

- Try this. Place your hand on your lower back while standing; now try and walk without moving your waist. If you did this properly you would have noticed how walking in this restricted way jammed up not just your back but your legs too.

- From doing this exercise you can imagine how such stiffness or restriction would affect the performance of your horse. The rider may know something is wrong, but it is quite hard to work out exactly what the problem is. I think the best way to help you to identify whether or not your horse has a problem (that is causing a decline in his performance, or preventing you from advancing any further) is to give you a few clues of possible causes.

WHAT TO LOOK FOR:

- Is it the saddle?

It is not the purpose of this book to discuss saddles and their fitting, except to say that poor or badly fitting saddles are often the cause of back problems. A qualified saddle fitter should regularly check your saddle. However, if while running your fingers down either side of your horse's spinous processes with quite a firm pressure he dips away, swishes his tail or puts his ears back then the saddle is quite likely to be the culprit.

● Is it the girth?

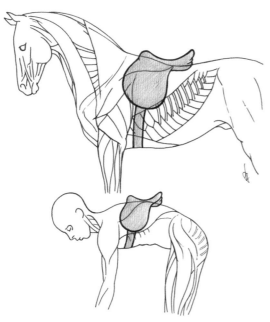

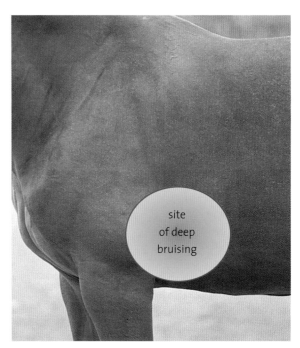

site of deep bruising

Comparative Exercise 4

● If you refer to the illustrations above, you will see that the girth sits over the horse's pectoral muscles and the upper portion of his ribcage. This is roughly where a bra sits on females, so this exercise is easier for females to understand. Try putting your index and second finger on your ribcage, then take a deep breath in, and you will feel your ribcage expand. Imagine wearing a rigid bra with no give or elastic in it, then consider the exertion a horse has to make while, say, jumping a fence. You can see why the ribcage must be able to expand in order to get enough air into the lungs to perform the given task. If there were no give in the material it would be quite a job to perform the task. Also, many dressage girths have the buckles low down, just about where the horse's elbow is and, as the horse's leg comes back towards the body, the buckles can interfere with the movement causing deep bruising to this area, which in turn will affect the horse's suspension.

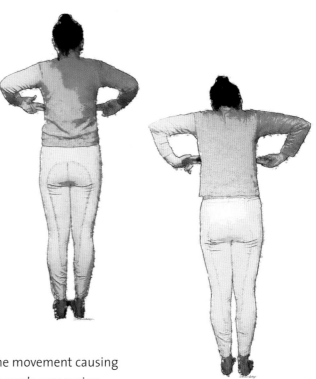

ANTERIOR AND POSTERIOR PECTORALS

Muscle action: To move the shoulder forward and foreleg inward. This muscle is bi-articular, which means it has a complex range of movement. It also serves to protect the scapular humeral joint and if chronic overuse is present will make a horse appear weight-bearing lame.

Problem: Mis-timing over fences; lack of range of movement at extended trot; losing ability over fences; shortened range of movement on forward stride on turning; refusing to take the correct lead.

> **CAUTION**
>
> Once again, this is a sensitive area. Respect your horse and apply light pressure to start with. Keep watching your horse to avoid a surprise nip!

Matthew has never liked having his girth done up! As you can see from his owner's face, this is his typical reaction. Because his pectoral muscles are contracted, his forward stride is very short.

Solution: Start by gently working in between the horse's forelegs using the heel of your hand in a circular motion (compressions). If your horse responds well to this, then you can start using cross-fibre friction. You should not need to work too long in this area as the muscles are very thin and sensitive; 2–3 minutes should be adequate on a daily basis until you see an improvement in performance. You can very carefully try a groomer here to see if your horse will tolerate it. Some horses love it, but others do not, so gently does it.

TIP

To speed up the healing process in this area, you can try using a girth sleeve.

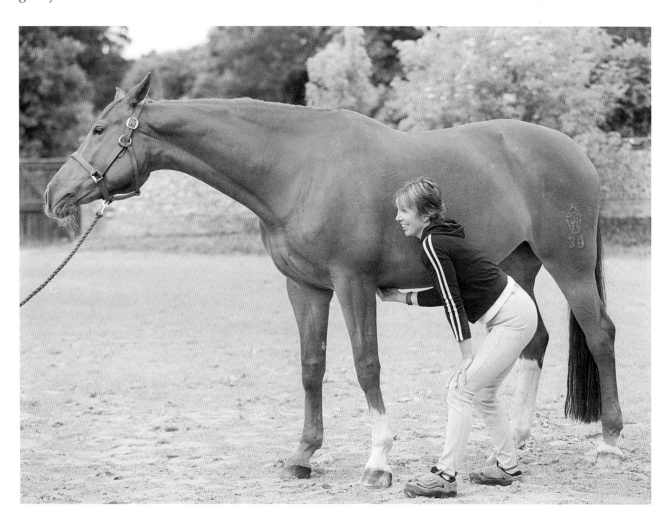

SERRATUS VENTRALIS
(Thoracic Part)

The serratus ventralis is a fan-shaped muscle which has two portions: a thoracic portion, which lies over the first nine ribs, and a cervical portion, which is in the neck. Both play a very important role in the suppleness and suspension of your horse.

Muscle action: To draw the forelegs back and flex the shoulder (the most important muscle for suspension in front). The muscle works in unison with the latissimus dorsi, so both groups must be worked together.

Problem: Losing suppleness in front and losing suspension; loss of range of movement through forelegs. If RSI is present, your horse will flinch away while pressure is applied around his girth area.

Solution: Start by using gentle friction in between the ribs, moving upwards towards the back of the shoulder blade where the bigger spasms are generally found. Finish off by using compressions. This should be done for 3–5 minutes per day per side until the range of movement improves.

CAUTION

Go easy. This is a sensitive area, particularly if you do have a girth problem. Respect what your horse is trying to tell you about how much pressure you can use.

TIP

Use your groomer in this area as it is usually tolerated well here. This is often an area where horses enjoy being treated, so if you are applying the right amount of pressure you will provoke a good reaction from your horse. He may even want to turn his head towards you and start grooming you!

TIP

You will often find the problem is worse on the nearside as this is the side that the buckles are done up on the girth.

ILIOCOSTALIS

Muscle action: Lateral flexion.

Lateral flexion is produced by the iliocostalis muscles, which lie roughly one third of the way down the horse's back. The horse is a prey animal and the muscles that produce sideways movements are relatively small. The reason why dressage horses are often more mature is that it takes a substantial amount of training for these muscles to produce the sustained power needed to perform many dressage movements, especially while carrying the weight of the rider. Think of dressage as a mixture of ballet and weight-lifting.

Problem: The horse's ribs seem to be stuck over to one side and he has more difficulty bending one way than the other.

Solution: Work along the entire length of the muscle. It starts under the shoulder blade so work in as close as you can behind the shoulder. I find using my thumbs or my first and second fingers easiest. This is quite a thin muscle and usually the biggest spasm will be found at the far end, against the last rib. Using cross-fibre friction, work on this area for about 5 minutes per day and a little longer and more vigorously on the side that he finds it harder to flex towards.

LATISSIMUS DORSI

Muscle action: To draw the foreleg back and flex the shoulder.

Problem: General lack of range of movement to forelegs; losing ability over fences.

Solution: Work the whole shoulder area along with the brachiocephalicus muscle and the omotransverse. Use deep compressions along the entire length of the muscle, followed by cross-fibre friction. Pay particular attention to the area just behind your horse's mane over the withers. Work daily until the condition improves.

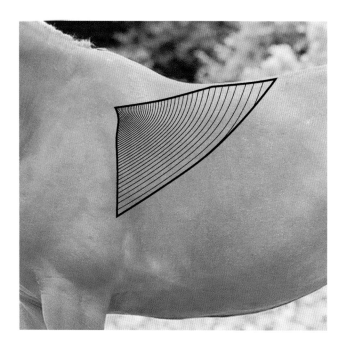

TIP

If this area is in spasm, using a good padded numnah usually helps, along with daily massage treatment. A groomer is usually well tolerated here.

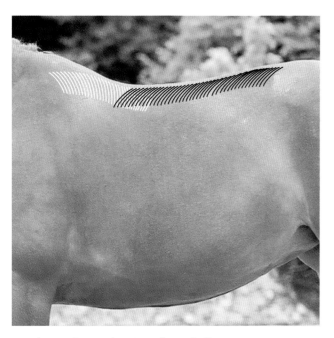

Hatching indicates direction of muscle fibres.

LONGISSIMUS DORSI

Muscle action: Back extensor and produces lateral flexion.

This muscle is possibly the most important one to you, the rider, as it is responsible for lifting the back, and thus providing engagement of the hindquarters. Any contraction in this muscle will affect both your horse's performance and power, yet it is one of the most common muscles to develop problems, and, as demonstrated in Comparative Exercise 1 (on page 12), if it is chronically contracted, a whole chain of difficulties results.

Problem: Finding engagement difficult; stiff, inflexible back; loss of ability over a fence; lateral work impaired; general loss of power from the hindquarters.

Solution: Start by using compression at the edge of the scapula, and continue over the back until you reach the start of the hindquarters. (This is where the muscle meshes with the gluteals and will make engagement of the hindquarters more difficult if contracted.)

Any juddering or shivering, particularly behind the saddle area, will mean that the muscle is highly contracted. Keep the compression slow if this is the case. Work up to cross-fibre friction if your horse will allow this. But, again, keep it slow if the back is juddering. Remember, deep contraction means that the muscles are more sensitive to pain – and if the area behind the saddle is affected, then your horse is suffering from low back pain, and just as in humans, he may be irritable, particularly if you work at a speed he doesn't like.

NOTE

This area may take quite some time to improve. Backs generally do.

The Neck and Poll

Comparative Exercise 5

- Try walking around while stiffening the base of your neck and you will see the effect it has on your shoulders: they become stiff, weak and ineffective.

BRACHIOCEPHALICUS AND OMOTRANSVERSE

Muscle action: To pull the foreleg forward and the neck down; lateral flexion of the neck.

This muscle is a very important one for riders and it must be soft in order for your horse to work in self-carriage. If this muscle is hard and/or overdeveloped, i.e. the horse has an 'upside down neck', it is almost certain that your horse is working on the forehand.

If, when you apply moderate pressure about two thirds of the way down the neck, your horse flinches or pulls back then your horse has an RSI.

Problem: Lack of range of movement to forelegs; loss of power over fences; stiff neck; neck carried to one side; horse's nose points in the opposite direction to the way you are going.

DOGGY PADDLE OR CRAWL?

Anyone who swims will know that the most powerful and effective stroke in swimming is the crawl. The powerful action of the shoulders propels the swimmer along as the arms come up and over the head. (This equates to 'working deep' in dressage.) However, if the brachiocephalicus muscle is stiff, the horse cannot use his shoulders properly. The only movement the horse can perform is the equine equivalent of doggy paddle, with the neck fixed and the jaw tight. This is highly ineffective in terms of propulsion as it takes a great deal of effort and places a lot of strain on the foreleg.

Poor Beer-Belly Horse has a stiff neck and gets exhausted from using himself in this way.

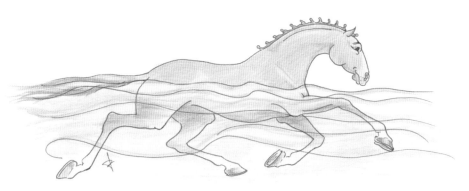

Our Gym Horse is using his whole body efficiently. His neck is lovely and soft, allowing energy to flow through his body.

Solution: Starting at the poll, use gentle compressions as you work towards the base of the neck. Try to increase the amount of pressure. If your horse is fine with this, continue by using cross-fibre friction. Again, start at the poll, gradually working down to the area where most stress build-up will be, which is about two-thirds of the way down the muscle. Do this along with the shoulder group of muscles daily until you feel an improvement in range of movement This muscle will only respond to treatment if the shoulders are treated at the same time.

TIP

You can try using the groomer here if the horse will tolerate it, as you will need to apply quite a firm pressure to be effective in treating this muscle.

SERRATUS VENTRALIS
(Cervical Part)

Muscle action: To act as main suspension muscle; will often be hardened in horses trained using draw reins incorrectly.

Problem: Losing ability over fences; loss of elasticity in any gait.

Solution: Start with gentle compressions, working up to cross-fibre friction if your horse tolerates it. Most horses enjoy groomers being used in this area.

TIP

Always check this muscle for hardening after jumping on hard ground.

TRAPEZIUS (Cervical Part) AND RHOMBOIDS

I have included these groups together as it is difficult to separate one group of muscles in this area for treatment.

Black hatching indicates the cervical portion of the trapezius, grey hatching indicates the thoracic part, and white shows the rhomboids.

Muscle action: The trapezius draws the shoulder up and forward; the rhomboids draw the foreleg back.

Problem: Loss of suspension; general poor quality of movement in front; mis-timing over jumps.

Solution: Start with compressions, concentrating on the area that is hardest to touch. In areas of deep spasm the muscle will judder (like an involuntary shiver). Build up to cross-fibre friction if your horse will tolerate it. Do this daily until the muscle appears softer and the range of movement improves.

NUCHAL LIGAMENT

Although, strictly speaking, this is not a muscle it plays an important part in the locomotion of the horse. Loss of suppleness to the neck portion of this ligament will result in poor head carriage and general lack of flexion through the neck. The ligament lies directly below the horse's mane and feels like a thick rope around 4–5 cms (about 2 inches) wide.

Problem: The horse finds it hard to flex his neck downwards from the base; he finds the 'seek response' difficult.

Solution: Start with compressions from the base of the neck working towards the poll, followed by cross-fibre friction concentrating on any areas of particular hardness.

This is a very tough bit of tissue and usually takes several weeks before you will see noticeable effects from your treatment.

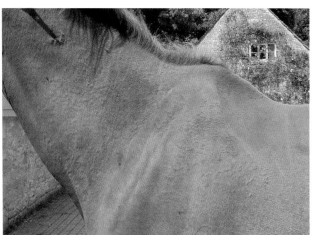

TIP

Check for unsightly rippling at the base of the neck (shown above). If present, it is generally a sign that at some point your horse has been trained using draw reins incorrectly.

The Hindquarters

The hindquarters are your horse's engine; they need to be powerful and free-moving. In horses working on the forehand, this is not the case. The muscles of the hindquarters transfer their movement to the hock joint, and when used correctly a reciprocal action occurs in the hock propelling the muscle mass forward. Where lack of engagement occurs, the main gluteal mass will look flat and the hamstring group will overdevelop. The hock will not articulate and will become stiff over time. Horses with this condition will often present with spavin-like symptoms as adhesions start to form in and around the hock joint.

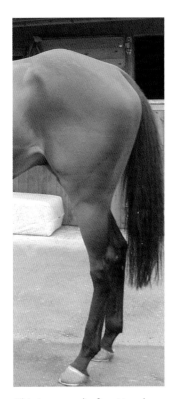

This is a very dysfunctional hindquarter – in fact this horse developed tendon problems in front as his shoulders were so contracted through overuse, and he eventually broke down.

CAUTION

Go easy to start with on any area in the hindquarters. If your horse is sore, his only way to let you know may be an instinctive reaction to pain: that is to kick the thing that is causing it!

Horses communicate very clearly!

BICEPS FEMORIS

Muscle action: To extend the hip, stifle and hock, and flex the caudal part of the stifle.

Problem: Hind leg toe-scuffs; lack of range of movement as hind leg moves forward.

Solution: Start at the top of the muscle, which you will find approximately 10 cms (4 inches) from the spinous processes. Work using compressions, with firm pressure to the base of the muscle, where you will often find the biggest areas of spasm. If your horse reacts well to this after a few minutes you can begin cross-fibre friction.

TIP

It is a good idea to check for heat here after a competition.

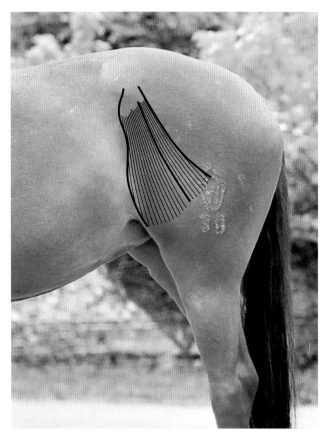

TENSOR FASCIA LATAE

Muscle action: To flex the hip and extend the stifle.

Problem: The hind leg extends away from the body on the forward stride on the affected side.

Solution: This is quite a tendinous muscle and therefore the blood supply is less, hence it tends to get RSIs quite often. Look for a tight little knot of tissue about halfway around the horse's hip joint and for general hard lines of fibrous tissue running towards the biceps femoris muscle. I find cross-fibre friction works best as this muscle is very fibrous, or use a groomer if your horse will permit it. Apply a vertical movement, crossing over the grain of the hard lines and fibrous tissue. Continue to treat the area until the fibrous look to the muscle diminishes.

ILIOPSOAS

Muscle action: To flex the hip.

Problem: Toe-scuffing; smaller range of movement to the affected hind leg; dropping hind leg over fences.

Solution: Look for a tight area of hardened muscle tissue on the lower portion of the hip (point of haunch). You may be able to feel the tension all the way to where it joins the femur (or thigh bone). Use cross-fibre friction over the whole area until you feel the muscle fibres beginning to soften. This may take a few treatments, as this is a tough, fibrous little muscle.

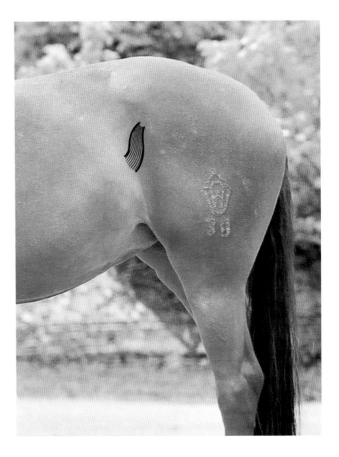

> **TIP**
>
> The iliopsoas is often a problem area in jumping horses.

> **CAUTION**
>
> Do not use your groomer here. It is a sensitive area, so go carefully.

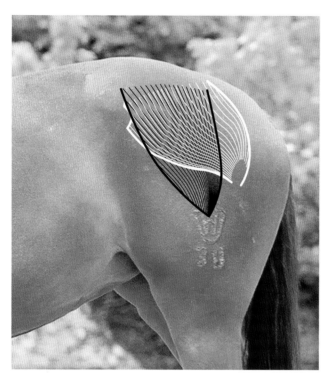

GLUTEUS (Medial and Superficial)

Muscle action: Forward movement of the hind leg; it flexes the hip and extends the stifle.

Problem: General back discomfort; lack of range of movement when hind leg forward moves forward.

Solution: Start using compressions over the entire area for 2–3 minutes, working up to cross-fibre friction if your horse tolerates it. Do this daily along with the tensor fascia latae until the condition improves.

Left: Hatching indicates direction of muscle fibres.

GASTROCNEMIUS

Muscle action: To extend the hock and flex the stifle. This is a very tendinous muscle and will take a lot of hard work if it is tight. (On a human, this lies roughly just above the Achilles' tendon, above the heel.)

Problem: Stifle/hock tightness.

Solution: Start by using your thumbs across the grain of the muscle tissue. If you find it interlaced with tight fibres that feel like piano wires (a term first used by my teacher and which I cannot better) and the tissue is hard, then you have a problem. This area is slow to respond to treatment and you will need patience, do a little bit every other day. If your horse responds well, try using a little more pressure until the condition improves.

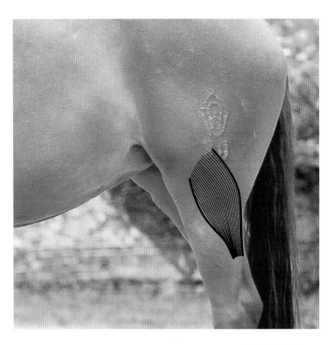

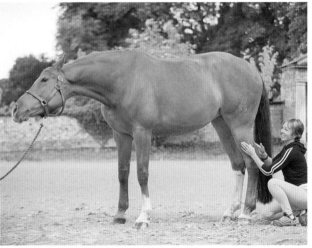

> **TIP**
>
> I usually find that if this muscle is tight there is nearly always a very poor quality to the action of the hock and it might be worth asking your vet whether a joint supplement might help. Sometimes, through releasing the muscles surrounding the hock a joint problem may be more noticeable. If this happens you must call your vet.

Comparative Exercise 6

 Try walking around while tensing your calf muscles and you will see how it affects your ankle (the human hock equivalent) to quite a degree. You can now see that if this muscle is tight, it will restrict the articulation of the hock.

> **CAUTION**
>
> Never start a treatment on this muscle without having treated the hindquarters first. If this muscle is sore your horse will have a very good way of letting you know – with its hooves! Do not use a groomer. It will be useful to have a friend watching to see what's happening up front and tell you which way your horse's ears are facing.

SEMITENDINOSUS

Muscle action: To extend the hip and hock and flex the stifle.

Problem: Loss of range of movement to the hind leg; losing the ability to track up. This muscle sits at the back of the thigh, just as it does on a human. Any of you who have had a torn hamstring will know how painful and debilitating it can be.

Comparative Exercise 6

- Go back to Comparative Exercise 1 (page 12), and bend over with locked knees. If there was an injury in this muscle you can imagine how painful it would be for a horse to move its legs further under its body.

TIP

It is a good idea to check for heat here after a competition and once your horse has cooled down. Once a hamstring muscle is injured it is very susceptible to re-injury if not given enough time to recover.

Solution: Start by applying a light pressure using compressions to the whole muscle. If your horse will tolerate it, use cross-fibre friction going across the muscle tissue.

CAUTION

If you find any tight lines running down the length of the muscle, be extra careful as this will mean it is in a high state of contraction. Go easy, keep an eye on your horse and carefully gauge the amount of pressure you can apply.

SEMIMEMBRANOSUS

Muscle action: To extend the stifle and the hip.

Problem: Loss of range of movement as hind leg moves forward; tracking inward on the forward stride, often with tail carriage to one side.

Solution: Start with a very gentle cupping movement using your whole hand, beginning under the top of the tail, gently pulling the muscle outwards away from the tail. Gradually work down towards the hock joint. While some horses love this, horses with contracted hamstrings will find it intolerable. If the muscle judders as you begin treatment, or if the horse swishes his tail and stamps his back leg, go very easy. It may take quite a few attempts before the horse is confident enough to allow you to work here.

Questions and Answers

Q. How often can I treat my horse?

A. Specific problems can be treated daily, but for short amounts of time – i.e. two to three minutes. All over sports massage should only be done about once a month to keep ahead of possible problems and to monitor muscle condition.

Q. Will my horse be sore after a treatment?

A. Only if you have applied too much pressure, but if you keep him on a loose rein while applying techniques, he can move off, and you can adjust your pressure to one that is more acceptable to him.

Q. My horse has small, round, swollen patches after I have treated him Why is this?

A. These are caused by toxins releasing through the skin's surface. The swellings usually go down after a few hours, however alarming they may appear. If they remain for longer than a few hours, consult your vet.

Q. Should my horse be exercised before I treat him?

A. No. This is generally not a good idea. Muscle tissue is dilated after exercise and therefore more delicate and susceptible to trauma. Wait until the horse has cooled down or, preferably, treat him before ridden work.

Q. How long should I leave it before I ride my horse once I have given him a treatment?

A. You should ride him as soon as you can. Sports massage prepares the muscles to work. If you do not have time to ride then, turn him out at the very least.

Q. How much pressure can I apply?

A. That is up to you and your horse, but if he is kept on a loose rein, the two of you will learn to gauge the right amount of pressure you can use, together. Every horse will be different.

Q. My horse seems to have gone lame after treatment. What have I done wrong?

A. Nothing, usually. This is normally an indication of a deeper problem at a structural level, i.e. the skeletal muscles will brace themselves in order to protect a joint under stress. If you loosen off the surrounding muscles, you may uncover a problem in the joint. If this happens, call your vet.

Q. When is the best time to treat my horse?

A. Pre-competition/pre-exercise.

Q. My horse seems to be ticklish and does not like being touched.

A. In my experience this is not usually ticklishness but contracted muscle tissue which has become sensitised to pain. Try working on another part of his body where he will allow you to touch him, and with patience, most horses will let you begin to work the affected area eventually. However, if he really does object and you are getting nowhere, don't risk being bitten or kicked. It can sometimes help to give him a haynet as a means of distraction.

Quick-Reference Guide to Specific Problems

- **Shortened or loss of range of movement to forelegs**
  Anterior and posterior pectorals, *page 34*
  Brachiocephalicus and omotransverse, *page 42*
  Deltoids, *page 30*
  Latissimus dorsi, *page 39*
  Serratus ventralis (thoracic part), *page 36*
  Trapezius (thoracic part) and rhomboids, *page 28*
  Trapezius (cervical part) and rhomboids, *page 46*
  Triceps, *page 29*

- **Losing ability over fences**
  Brachiocephalicus and omotransverse, *page 42*
  Deltoids, *page 30*
  Iliopsoas, *page 51*
  Latissimus dorsi, *page 39*
  Longissimus dorsi, *page 40*
  Serratus ventralis (both parts), *pages 45 and 36*
  Trapezius (thoracic part) and rhomboids, *page 28*

- **Lateral work lacks range of movement**
  Anterior and posterior pectorals, *page 34*
  Biceps femoris, *page 49*
  Iliopsoas, *page 51*
  Iliocostalis, *page 38*
  Supraspinatus and infraspinatus, *page 31*
  Latissimus dorsi, *page 39*
  Longissimus dorsi, *page 40*

- **Mis-timing over fences**
  Tensor fascia latae, *page 50*
  Trapezius (cervical part) and rhomboids, *page 46*

- **Stiff back/finding engagement difficult**
  Gluteus (medial and superficial), *page 52*
  Longissimus dorsi, *page 40*
  Latissimus dorsi, *page 39*

- **Problem in bending to one direction**
  Iliocostalis, *page 38*
  Longissimus dorsi, *page 40*

- **Ribs stuck to one side**
  Iliocostalis, *page 38*

- **Losing suspension**
  Serratus ventralis (thoracic part), *page 36*
  Trapezius (cervical part) and rhomboids, *page 46*

- **Losing suppleness in front**
  Serratus ventralis (cervical part), *page 45*
  Serratus ventralis (thoracic part), *page 36*

- **Loss of power from hindquarters**
  Gluteus (medial and superficial), *page 52*
  Longissimus dorsi, *page 40*
  Semimembranosus, *page 55*
  Semitendinosus, *page 54*

- **Stiff neck**
  Brachiocephalicus and omotransverse, *page 42*
  Nuchal ligament, *page 47*

- **Neck to one side**
  Brachiocephalicus and omotransverse, *page 42*

- *Nose pointing opposite direction*
  Brachiocephalicus and omotransverse, *page 42*

- *Loss of elasticity at all paces*
  Serratus ventralis (cervical part), *page 45*
  Serratus ventralis (thoracic part), *page 36*
  Trapezius (thoracic part) and rhomboids, *page 28*

- *'Seek response' difficult*
  Nuchal ligament, *page 47*
  Brachiocephalicus and omotransverse, *page 42*

- *Hind-leg toe-scuffs*
  Biceps femoris, *page 49*
  Iliopsoas, *page 51*

- *Lack of range of movement to hind leg*
  Biceps femoris, *page 49*
  Tensor fascia latae, *page 50*

- *Hind leg extends away from body*
  Tensor fascia latae, *page 50*

- *Stifle hock tightness*
  Biceps femoris, *page 49*
  Gastrocnemius, *page 53*

- *Losing ability to track up*
  Longissimus dorsi, *page 40*
  Semitendinosus, *page 54*

- *Tracking in on forward stride*
  Semimembranosus, *page 55*

- *Tail carriage to one side*
  Semimembranosus, *page 55*

- *Falling in/falling out*
  This is usually a complex problem having one or more of many causes. Each case should be assessed separately.

Glossary

Articulate – joint to move through full range.

Caudal – furthest towards the tail.

Dishing – foreleg is thrown outward with each stride.

Engagement – when the power of the horse's movement comes from behind.

Extension – horse covers as much ground as possible with each stride, lengthening his stride and his frame at the same time.

Extensor – lengthens the muscle.

Flexion – bending.

Flexor – shortens the muscle.

Gaits – paces that the horse works at, namely walk, trot, canter and gallop.

Lateral – sideways.

Leads – this indicates the horse's leading leg in canter, e.g. on the right rein he should lead with his right foreleg. If he prefers to lead with the opposite leg this may indicate a problem.

Protruberance – prominent, used to describe a bone, e.g. point of hip.

'Seek response' – when the horse is stretching down – i.e. working long and low while the rider maintains a contact.

Self-carriage – horse carries himself in balance without leaning on the rider's hand for support.

Suspension – the phase in trot and canter during which the horse has no feet on the ground.

Top-line – muscles lying either side of the spinous processes.

Tracking up – when the hind feet step into the tracks of the forefeet.